Contents

Words in **bold** can be found in the glossary on page 23.

A snowy day

Do you like playing in the snow on a winter's day? Snow is brilliant for making snowballs. Snow is great for going **tobogganing**.

What is snow?

But snow can make life hard for animals and people. Animals can find it hard to get enough food. Cars and lorries get stuck in deep **snow drifts**.

Snow is made from tiny **crystals** of **ice**.
The crystals stick together to make
snowflakes. Every snowflake has six sides.
But there are lots of different shapes
and patterns.

Snow falls from the clouds.
It settles in layers on the ground.
There are different kinds of snow.
Wet, heavy snow is good for
making snowmen.

Trees and plants in the snow

Trees and plants have special ways of living in the snow. Conifer trees have a sloping shape. The snow slides off the branches without breaking them.

Some plants have hairy petals and leaves. These keep the plants warm when it snows. This edelweiss plant grows high up in the snowy **Alps** mountains.

Animals in the snow

The polar bear lives in the freezing cold **Arctic**. Its thick fur coat keeps it snug and warm. Baby polar bears are born in a cosy den dug in the snow.

In winter, Arctic foxes grow white fur coats to match the colour of the snow. Their coats help to hide them from hungry enemies, such as polar bears!

Wrapping up warm

People need to wrap
up warm on a
snowy day. A thick
coat and hat will keep out
the cold. Boots will help you to walk
through the snow without slipping over.

The Inuit are people who live in the **Arctic**. They wear coats and boots made from animal fur. Fur is very good for keeping out the cold.

Living in the snow

This is an Inuit town in Greenland. The houses are small because big houses are hard to keep warm. Their windows are sealed shut to keep out the cold. They are built close together to shelter each other from the icy wind.

The Chukchi people in Siberia look after herds of reindeer. The Chukchi eat reindeer meat and use reindeer skins for making tents and clothes.

Snowstorms

A fierce snowstorm is called a **blizzard**. It happens mostly in winter. Strong winds blow the snow around making it difficult to see to walk or drive.

In a blizzard, the roads get blocked with snow. This machine is called a **snowplough**. It is used to clear the roads. It pushes the snow to the side of the road.

Snow danger

Sometimes a thick layer of loose snow crashes down a mountain. This is called an **avalanche**. The snow can bury people, houses and animals on its way.

Trained rescue dogs sniff
for people buried in the
snow. Then rescuers dig
to help get the people out.

Sports in snow

Snow can be dangerous but it can also be fun. This boy is **snowboarding**. He is wearing specially padded clothes to stop him from getting hurt if he falls over.

Layers of dry, powdery snow are great for skiing. Top skiers can race down the mountains at very fast speeds. They use ski poles to help them keep their balance.

Snow fact file

- Millions and millions of snowflakes have fallen to earth. Most of them have six sides. But every single snowflake has a different shape. You never get two the same.

- Paradise, Mount Rainier, USA is one of the snowiest places on earth. Between 1971 and 1972, more than 30 metres of snow fell.

- Snow doesn't just fall in cold places. The top of Mount Kilimanjaro in Africa is always covered in snow, even though it is hot at the bottom. This is because it gets colder the higher you go, so snow is more likely.

- In September 1981, snow fell in the Kalahari Desert in Africa. No one could remember it snowing there before.

Glossary

Alps Some high mountains in Europe.

Arctic The area around the North Pole.

avalanche A thick layer of snow that suddenly slides down a mountainside.

blizzard A very fierce snowstorm with heavy snow and strong winds.

crystals Tiny pieces of ice.

ice Frozen water.

snowboarding Sliding over the snow with both of your feet on a board.

snow drifts When the wind blows the snow into deep piles or mounds.

snowplough A machine that is used to clear snow from the roads.

tobogganing Sliding across the snow on a sledge, or toboggan.

Index

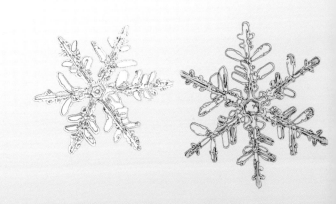